THIS uncover& discover BOOK BELONGS TO

• • • • • • • • • • • • • • • • •

WALKER BOOKS

Here's a hungry chameleon.

Here's a
juicy grasshopper...

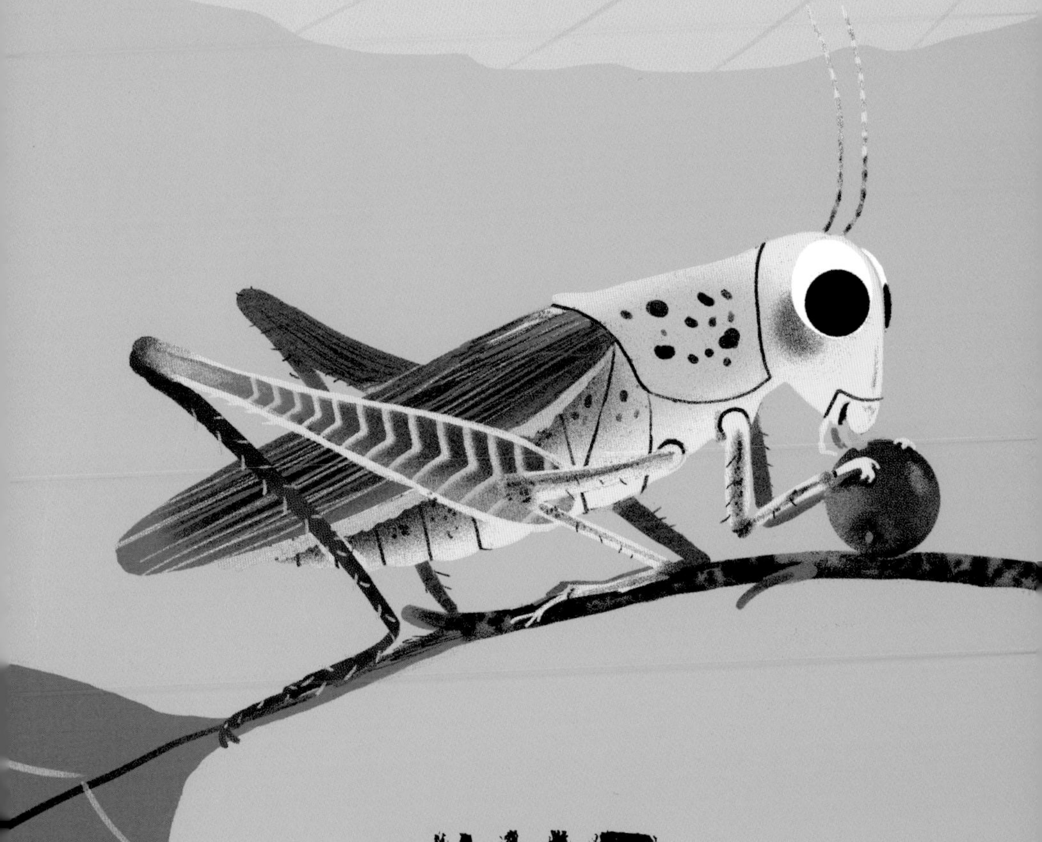

WHAT
HAPPENS
NEXT?

The chameleon shoots out his long, long tongue ...

and the sticky end
catches the grasshopper.

THWAP!

Then he pulls in
his tongue, like he's
sucking spaghetti.

YUM.

Here's a beaver
who needs a home.

Here is a pile of sticks
and mud he has gathered.

WHAT HAPPENS NEXT?

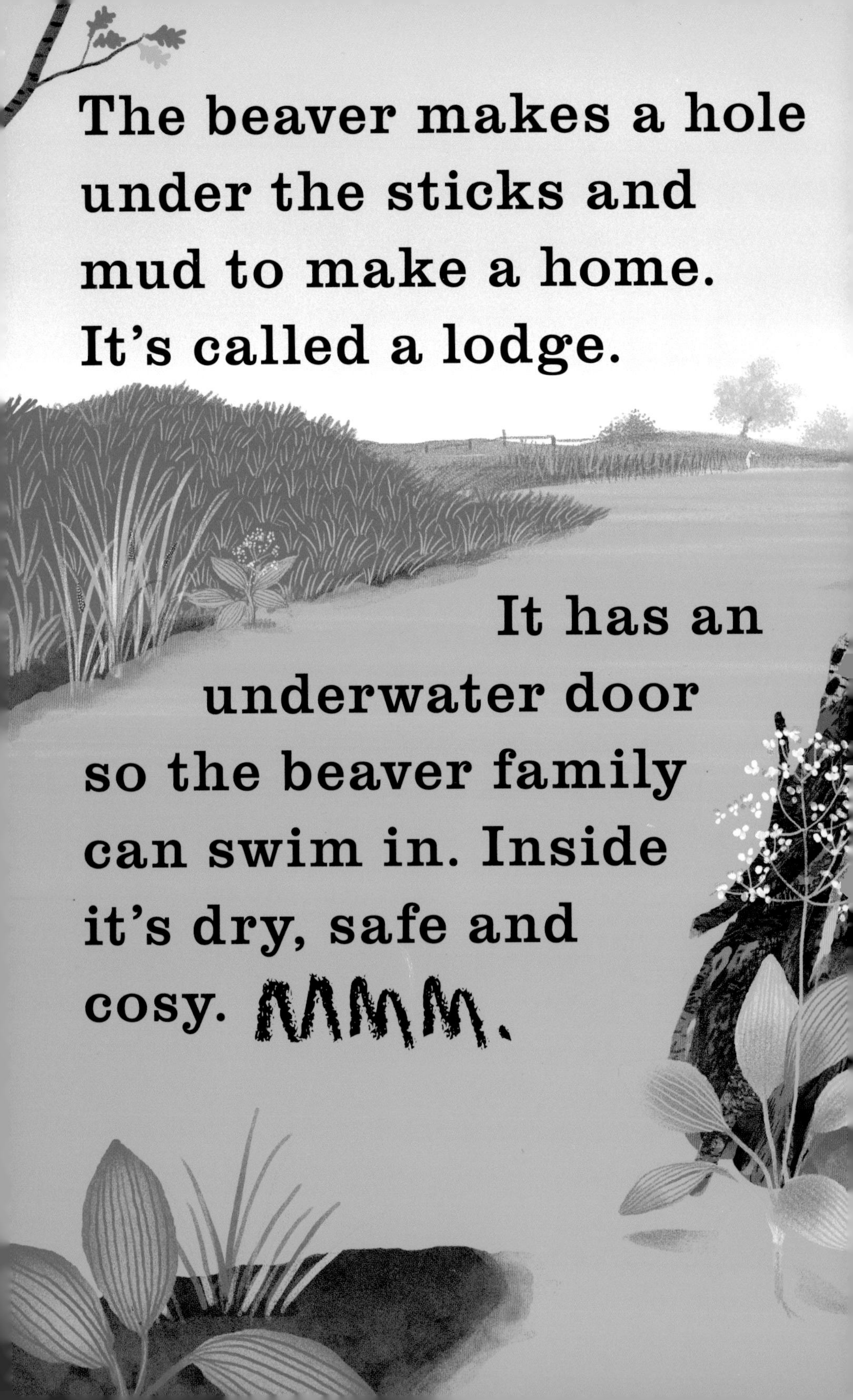

The beaver makes a hole under the sticks and mud to make a home. It's called a lodge.

It has an underwater door so the beaver family can swim in. Inside it's dry, safe and cosy. MMMM.

Here's a peacock who needs a wife. He wants to get the peahen to notice him.

Here's a peahen
who's looking
the other way.

WHAT HAPPENS
NEXT?

The peacock opens his beautiful tail and shakes his feathers so they shimmer and shine. He opens his beak –

SCREEECH!

Now she's looking at him!

Here's a honey bee
who's found a lovely
patch of flowers.

Here's a hive full of her relations who don't know where it is.

WHAT HAPPENS NEXT?

The honey bee goes back to the hive and does a wiggly dance that tells the other bees where the flowers are.

They fly straight to the flowers, to collect sweet nectar for making into honey.

Here are two chimps
who want some food.

Here's a mound full of tasty termites – but it's hard as rock.

WHAT HAPPENS NEXT?

Mama chimp pokes
a twig through a tiny
hole in the mound and

the termites cling to it.
She and her baby lick
the termites off. YUM!

Can you match the pictures to help you remember what happened?

First published 2012 by Walker Books Ltd
87 Vauxhall Walk, London SE11 5HJ

1 3 5 7 9 10 8 6 4 2

This book has been typeset in Print, Clarendon T and Eraser

Printed in China

British Library Cataloguing in Publication Data: a catalogue record for this book is available from the British Library.

ISBN 978-1-4063-2810-3

www.walker.co.uk